HEALING GRIEF

by
Amy Hillyard Jensen

ISBN 0-934230-08-0

See rear cover for ordering information.

Acknowledgment: The author expresses her thanks to the many reviewers of the manuscript, both lay and professional, who, by their thoughtful criticism, helped significantly in developing the final text. A special thanks is extended to those still grieving who took the time and trouble to offer suggestions.

A PERSONAL MESSAGE

Someone you love very much has died. The pain and fear wash over you in waves.

You may feel that you cannot bear it. You wonder if you will survive. It is true that everything will be changed. You will remember and grieve a little all the rest of your life. From my own experience, however, I can tell you that you have more strength, more resources than you realize. You *can* make it through the valley.

When our nine-year-old Michael drowned, I grieved much and for a long time. Then, eight years later, the unthinkable happened—something that I had prayed to be spared, that I felt I could not possibly endure...I lost another child. Twenty-three-year-old Eric was killed in an auto accident.

Through these two deaths I learned some of the things this booklet will describe. I also became a student, through books and seminars, of those who have studied grief. And I learned more through sharing the burden of other bereaved parents, husbands, wives, and children.

I believe, therefore, that I can help you. No one can tell you, of course, how long or in what manner you "should' grieve—your grief is unique. But there are elements of bereavement that are more or less common to all who pass through it. Understanding these common elements and how others have dealt with them can be of great help.

CONTENTS

SHOCK

Your first response to your loss might be what is sometimes called shock. A kind of numbness envelops you. It's nature's insulation, cushioning the blow.

And it's physical. You might experience odd physical sensations like I did—a spaced-out feeling, a knot in my stomach, no appetite.

Your mind might do strange things. A few hours after Michael drowned, I was distressed to discover a button missing on my sweater. A little later the incongruity hit me—I had lost a son and was worrying about a button.

But the shock, the numbness, will not prevent you from doing what you must do.

If you are a mother who must cope with the needs of a young family after the death of their father, you will manage somehow to meet those needs. You will act, at least in part, instinctively.

If you are a husband and father, upon whose shoulders a great weight seems to have fallen, you too will manage.

Whatever your situation you will retain the capacity to be rational. The numbness will soon wear away, and *real* grieving will begin.

DENIAL

Hard on the heels of shock comes denial. You comprehend intellectually what has happened, but on a deeper level all of your habits and memories are denying death. You will find yourself setting the wrong number of plates at the dinner table or saving bits of news for someone who will never be able to hear them.

Your dreams may reveal the conflict. In one of my dreams, friends tried to convince me that my son was dead and that I was wrong to "hold on to him." I kept insisting he was alive.

The depth of your denial may depend on how much you need your loved one to be alive. A friend of mine was left with five young children when her husband was killed. Tragic enough, but she was a polio victim, and her husband's support had been extraordinary. During the early hours of her grief, she cried over and over, "It couldn't have been him. There must be some mistake!"

Denial may remain in some form for months or years, and there is no required schedule for getting rid of it. Some people consistently stay away from the grave. Some leave the deceased's room unchanged for quite a while. Do what feels right for you as you gradually move toward acceptance. For most of us, keeping a few treasures and pictures in view indefinitely is not a denial, but an affirmation of love. Those who would not allow you that privilege just haven't been there!

In time you will find that you can face reality. Though a part of you will always grieve, you will be able to accept the death.

THE FIRST FEW DAYS

While you are in the first numbing hours of grief, there is much activity. Friends and relatives are coming. Others are telephoning. Flowers are arriving. Women are bringing dishes of food and giving a quick hug. Men are coming solemnly, struggling with their emotions. Funeral plans are being made. The activity seems outside of yourself. You go through it all in a kind of dream.

All of this activity can be helpful. It might relieve a little of the intensity of your bereavement. David, our eldest son, furiously mowed the lawn soon after Eric's death mostly because, I believe, the vigorous activity helped relieve some of his anger and grief.

Visitors. Although condolence calls are a dreaded duty for many, they are made out of love and concern. Even the most awkward expressions of sympathy can be accepted with that in mind.

If people offer to help, which they will, let them. Suggest things they might do. Friends helped us in many ways. Some met relatives at the airport. One notified neighbors and certain out-of-touch friends. Another did my hair in my home. A neighbor hosted out-of-town relatives. And others helped with housekeeping chores.

Accept help from the professionals. Funeral directors, pastors, and others are ready to guide you and to help you make decisions.

Preparation for Burial. There are decisions to make and tasks to do...a casket to select, clothing to prepare...duties which are not only necessary (unless there is direct cremation, which is discussed below) but also therapeutic. Although painful, they are part of the process needed for grief to heal—it's better to be involved than shielded. One mother I know chose her own special involvement. She sat by her dead child's casket and sang him a lullaby for the last time. In earlier days, family members often dressed the body. Although most of us are not prepared for such participation, it can be arranged if desired.

Viewing and Touching the Body. Especially if death came suddenly, viewing and touching the body can be a part of the healing process. It may involve more pain, and it should not be forced. But seeing the body may be the beginning of facing reality, for there is nothing so empty looking as a body from which the essence of life has vanished. Touching, too, may be a needed expression of love.

Viewing by Young Children. Should young children be allowed to view the body? Some people don't think so. But loving and careful consideration should be given to the individual child. The child's grief and needs may be as great as yours, and his bewilderment even greater. Generally, let him look *(1) if he wants to,* and *(2) if he can understand a simple explanation of what to expect.*

> We were uncertain whether six-year-old Demeree should see her brother in the "slumber room." I told her she could come with the family and we would decide later. As we stood around Michael's small casket, Demeree gradually crept forward and peeked. Quiet tears rolled down her cheeks. Later she said she should have brought her hankie. I mistakenly said, "I wouldn't have let you see him if I had known it would make you cry." "No," she replied, "I *wanted* to see him. I just wish I had brought my hankie."

Planning the Funeral. To many people, the funeral service is a terrible ordeal to be gotten over as quickly as possible, and you may be one of those who wants little or no service. Such is your privilege, of course. Consider, however, that a service tends to benefit the survivors, most of whom will receive some healing from it.

A funeral or memorial service can do more. It brings the *support* of friends and community. It gives you a *goal,* a stabilizing objective in those first uncharted, emotional days. And it provides for a last, loving tribute, a public *declaration of love.*

Be involved in the planning if you can. Choosing music and speakers brings a sense of control and makes the service more meaningful. It is better to have an old friend speak with tears than an unknown clergyman speak with eloquence. If you limit the time for each, more than one speaker can be used. Before sheduling the service, be sure the speaker or speakers have been contacted and are available.

Consider participation by family members. Occasionally a mourner is sufficiently controlled to be in the service. There could have been no more loving tribute to my son Eric than the clear, strong voices of his three brothers singing one of his favorites, John Denver's "Sunshine."

Cremation is an option now widely used, often because it lowers cost. If state law permits, the ashes may be scattered in a meaningful location, giving comfort to the survivors. But there are some cautions. If there is *direct* cremation with no family viewing of the body and no physical contact, accepting the death can be more difficult. This is especially true for children and older adults. Family viewing can be arranged through the hospital or mortician. And a memorial service, you might decide, could still be desirable.

ANGER

Anger is a normal response. You may have it in any degree from mild to raging, depending on your personality and the circumstances. You may find yourself angry at the physicians and nurses for not saving your loved one, or, if there was an accident, at the one who caused it. You may even be angry at the one who died. A widow is often angry at her husband for "deserting" her. If he neglected his health, the anger may be greater.

God gets a lot of blame. Even agnostics may say, "What kind of God would let this happen?" When Michael drowned, I felt that God had let me down.

And I was angry at my husband. He was supposed to be watching—why hadn't he been more careful? Terrible grief demands a scapegoat. But no hidden animosities arose, as they often do, to reinforce this anger, and it was resolved in time. Even good marriages, however, can suffer from the stress of anger (see page 16).

Important: Anger needs to be expressed. One person screams in a private place. Another beats a mattress with a piece of hose. Another does hard exercise. Everyone should at least talk about it. Bottling up anger causes stress, and the cork tends to come off in one way or another, often affecting job performance and other relationships.

Like other phases of grief, anger may come and go. If it seems destructive or prolonged, consider professional help.

GUILT

Few survivors escape without some feeling of guilt. You may feel guilty because you did not make sure your spouse took care of his health or got to the doctor sooner. A long illness may have led to a feeling of resentment and consequently guilt over the resentment. A sudden or accidental death may give rise to the torture of all kinds of *"if only's."*

A mother was suffering months of anguish because she had not checked the back door of her car. The older children told her it was locked. Somehow it was not, and her precious toddler fell out and was killed. Eventually she developed an outlook I believe helpful to anyone who feels his neglect contributed to a death.

"I asked myself," she told me, "if I had my child back, could I promise that I would never make another mistake? I knew I could not make that promise."

Nobody can. If the day you would like to change could be undone, what about the *next* day? It might bring some other situation, some other failure, equally as devastating.

The terrible tragedy of suicide is compounded by excessive guilt feelings. Often friends and community are not supportive and may blame you, quite unfairly, for not doing more to prevent the death. The fact is that you probably did everything you could think of doing. In the final analysis, you cannot *control* the behavior of another person, even your own child. But the complexity of the suicide problem may be more than you can handle alone. Consider professional help if you are burdened by guilt.

Whatever your situation, realize that feelings of guilt and regret are normal. Meet them and dispose of them. Accept your fallibility. Get professional counseling if needed. Consider also that a clergyman might be able to help you deal with guilt on a spiritual level.

DEPRESSION

When numbness wears off and rage has been exhausted, depression may arrive. Three weeks after Michael's death, while I was on a family camping trip, lethargy and despair took over. I simply sat—nothing could rouse me. I *willed* Mike to be there, but all was emptiness.

The ones who "take it so well" tend to hit bottom later. A hopeless feeling pervades. Mornings are terrible...a supreme act of will is needed just to pull yourself out of bed. TV dinners are the rule. Conversation and shopping are an exhausting chore.

This is the time when you need a friend, someone who will listen and not judge, someone who will allow your *rambling* and *repetitive* talk about your loss.

A friend can also help to get you into *activity,* some diversion for mind and body. I could not bear the frenzy of most television, but participation in a choral group was helpful. Consider sports activity or anything soothing and physical. But avoid frantic activity—it's like running away, and you need to face reality.

Sometimes, in cases of unusually intense or prolonged grief, physicians prescribe an antidepressant drug. As a temporary measure, this may help you to face your grief and begin to work through it. But beware of masking reality. If medication becomes more than a temporary measure, you should also be getting professional counseling.

Most people recover slowly but surely. The down times will come again and again, but not as often and without staying as long as in the beginning. It's a long process, sometimes taking years, but healing comes. It will come for you.

CHILDREN

Children know sorrow. Who can say that they suffer less than adults? Sometimes the hurt goes deeper. In any event, they have needs that should not be overlooked.

How do you tell a child that someone he loved has died? It's difficult, but being straightforward is the best rule. Tell the truth. Handled carefully, the truth should be good enough. Your own beliefs will of course determine what you say about the meaning of death and about life after death. And you can admit there is much more that you do not know. But distortions of reality can do lasting harm. For example, "gone to sleep" may lead to a fear of going to sleep, and "God took her" may lead to a hatred of God for being cruel. Incidentally, death in a hospital may lead to a fear of hospitals unless the child is reassured.

Your assurance of love and support is the greatest thing you can do for a grieving child. He should be reminded that the loss of one important relationship of love does not mean the loss of others, including the one with you. *And he should understand he is in no way to blame for the death.* Young children often think that anything "bad" that happens in their little world is somehow their fault. A very young child may wonder, *"Who will take care of me?"* Assure him that his physical needs will be met.

Let the child participate in the family sorrow. If shielded, he may feel rejected, as though he does not belong. He needs you, and you need him. *Let the child see your grief.* It may be distressing to see Father cry, but it's far more distressing to see "business as usual."

Protect the child from unnecessary burdens. Do not say, or let others say, to the child who has lost a father, "You are the man of the house, now." And no child (or adult) should be told to "be brave." Having to put up a false front makes grieving more difficult.

Let the child express his feelings. It's all right for the child to be angry. But do not probe. Provide the environment in which feelings can be expressed spontaneously. If more than one child is involved, spend time alone with each. The needs of one may be much greater than the needs of others, as was the case with our ten-year-old Leslie. She lost her best friend when Michael died. Looking back, I can see that her father and I should have spent more time with her.

Be aware that tears are not the only measure of grief. Unfortunately the crying child gets the most sympathy. The less demonstrative child will also need your attention.

Let the child share in your progress. As you work through grief, coming to terms with your loss, your child will be helped to do the same. Find, if you can, some activities you can do together, and share your involvement with friends, family, church, and community.

SILENCE

There seems to be a taboo in our society against speaking of death. Co-workers tend to avoid you. Friends seem in unnatural haste when they happen to meet you in a store. Even family members have difficulty. Often the motive is to protect you from the pain of remembering, but the pain of loneliness and isolation is worse.

My own father demonstrated this problem whenever he and my stepmother visited in the early days after Michael's death. At times I would say something like, "That reminds me how Mike and Leslie used to...." Such a remark was always met by an awkward silence and a change of subject.

The child who has lost one parent may be strangely non-communicative with the surviving parent and may do better with a friend or sibling. But if the parent can create comfortable times alone with the child, the words may come.

A husband and wife may not be able to speak easily to each other about their loss, partly because they are likely to grieve differently. Accept the difference. Nonetheless, with both child and spouse, there must be conversation about the deceased and the death. It's vital for healing the sorrow, and it's vital for the marriage—see page 16.

As to the friend who cannot seem to talk to you, help bridge the awkwardness. I went out of my way to talk to acquaintances, showing that I wore no black "D" embroidered on my shirt. Thereafter they greeted me without strain.

For the most helpful conversation, however, you need to find a special friend, a professional counselor, a spiritual counselor, or a group of bereaved people like yourself. *Compassionate Friends* (see last page) is an organization of bereaved parents who get together to share and talk out grief over the loss of a child. There is an organization of widows—*Widowed Lifeline*—in my area; perhaps there is something similar in yours. Expressing feelings to one who knows your experience brings remarkable relief.

TEARS

Perhaps you cannot cry. A man reared in the typical masculine image often does not. But tears are usually a necessary release. Repressed grief may lead to psychological harm and physical illness.

Most people who do not cry are so busy "hanging on" that they won't let their minds come to grips with their loss. They are in effect still *denying*.

One possible solution is to deliberately take time to grieve. Review mementos. Play nostalgic music. Look at pictures and read old letters. One therapist often recommends one hour a day—a grieving prescription.

The seeming strength of the stiff upper lip is not helpful to others either. Crying helps others to see your love and is a healthy model for children. One of my sons vividly recalled his father's behavior after Michael drowned: "You started to cry and cry. I'd never seen you cry before. It made me realize how much you loved us all." Eight years later when Eric died, each of the brothers, now grown and married, was able to express his grief in tears, possibly helped by his father's example.

When both a husband and wife are grieving, as in the death of a child, the husband may feel he must play the Stoic, the strong one who consoles his wife. He may manage for a time, then wonder, "Doesn't anyone care how I feel?"

If the husband remains strong and silent, scheduled talk sessions may help to bring both tears and words (see next section). Often a father still cannot cry or talk about the child or the death, and that may simply have to be accepted. The wife should use others for her sounding board.

But show whatever love and affection you can. The lack of tears can be understood and allowed for, and the marriage can go on.

MARRIAGE AND THE DEATH OF A CHILD

If you have lost a child, your marriage is likely to be severely strained. The anticipated ideal of each spouse supporting and helping the other is rarely realized in the death of a child. Overwhelmed with grief, neither husband nor wife is in a position to be leaned upon. Do not expect that your spouse will understand completely or solve your grief—each has a special path of grief to follow.

Accusations of Guilt. Nothing is so devastating to the marriage of bereaved parents as *blame.* If you feel that your spouse is responsible for the child's death, such as by not giving sufficient care, your marriage situation is probably precarious. Few grieving parents can handle the accusation of guilt. So *do not accuse.* Neither let your feelings smoulder unexpressed. Instead get into dialogue with an outside party—a psychiatrist, pastor, or other counselor.

Communication. Often one spouse, or both, cannot seem to talk about the child. Scheduling a certain daily time for such talk has been the answer for many. At least the non-talking parent can *listen* during those periods and may talk eventually. Communication in general needs to be kept going too. Beware of harboring little grievances. Talk about them before you have a whole bag full.

Other Problems. A long illness may have left *financial difficulties* that only a debt counselor can solve. The continued absence of *sexual relations* desperately needs resolution. A *malaise* about the marriage may set in, coloring everything. All kinds of *resentments and recriminations* may surface.

Help, Help! If you have any of these problems and no resolution is in process, outside help is urgently needed. With your emotions so intense, what hope is there for clear vision and objectivity on your own? Find a counselor or social worker experienced in grief counseling. Get with a group, such as Compassionate Friends. Don't lose both your child and your marriage.

FAITH

Faith in God will help. That's not simply my opinion. Researchers in death and dying have discovered that faith is a powerful aid in coping with bereavement. If you have spiritual roots, you are likely to pass more easily through the process of grief and may even avoid some phases altogether.

Perhaps your faith is tentative and untested. You can, nonetheless, build on such faith as you have. You can doubt your doubts. You can begin to lean on the promises of Scripture, both as to life after death for your loved one and help in your own grief. Consider, for example, this promise of God from the Hebrew and Christian Scriptures:

> The Lord is near to the broken hearted and saves those who are crushed in spirit. Ps. 34:18.

You can, like I, experience a sense of transcendent love, which I believe is from God. The night after Michael's death I lay in bed, too sad and exhausted to sleep. Gradually a strong, sweet spirit came over me. I felt like I was saying goodbye to my little boy. I had never felt closer to him. And I was feeling not mainly sorrow or shock—I was feeling love.

That transcendent feeling of love carried me through those first few difficult weeks. Others describe similar experiences. Catherine Marshall in *To Live Again,* speaks of a "Presence." Others speak of the "Comforter."

The experience of love and assurance is sometimes delayed until months of anguish have passed. But I believe it is God's gift to everyone who earnestly seeks him.

Exercise such faith as you have. Study the promises of the Bible (examples: Psalm 55:22, Romans 8:38-39). Pray. God, who knows your grief (Exodus 3:7), will give you the strength you need, which for now, is simply the strength to go from one day to the next.

GROWTH

Time alone will not heal grief. You have to deal with it, to work through it. In the process you can actually transmute grief into personal growth. You can become something *more* than you were. Consider the following ideas.

Build on your memories. Though you must accept your loved one's death, you need not sever all ties. You can use memories to establish a new kind of relationship, and you can find ways for those memories to enrich your life.

Many survivors become more involved in their loved one's work or interest. A spouse can sometimes take part in a husband's or wife's business. In our family there was an intense interest in preserving Eric's music, with each brother and sister developing his own musical talent and often singing "Eric's songs."

If you have literary ability, you might write in a way that is influenced by or dedicated to the memory of the one you loved. If you have the money, consider setting up a memorial fund or foundation.

Recall the humorous times and laugh about them. Some will disapprove if you laugh "too soon," but it's not disrespectful. Remembering with laughter is helpful.

Assist other bereaved people. Find an organization through which you can be a friend to the sorrowing.

Building on memories *directly* is not the only way to go. Realize that you may be at a kind of crossroads where new opportunities for service or involvement should be explored. This may be the time to become active in church, return to school, work with needy children, or volunteer at a hospital.

Whatever you do, do not waste your life in unproductive sorrow. The best memorial to a loved one is a full, *growing* life.

GUIDELINES

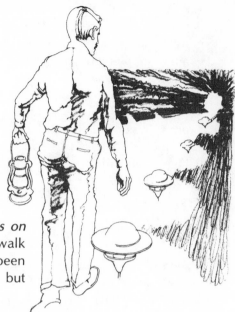

Here are 15 *lamps on the path,* lights to walk by. Several have been mentioned before but bear repeating.

1. *Accept the grief.* Roll with the tides of it. Do not try to be "brave." Take time to cry. This also applies to men...strong men can and do cry.

2. *Talk about it.* Share your grief *within the family*—do not attempt to protect them by silence. *Find a friend to talk to,* someone who will listen without passing judgment. If possible, find someone who has experienced a similar sorrow. And talk often. If the friend tells you to "snap out of it," find another friend.

3. *Keep busy.* Do purposeful work that occupies the mind, but avoid frantic activity.

4. *Take care of yourself.* Bereavement can be a threat to your health. At the moment you may feel that you don't care. That will change. You are important—your life is valuable—care for it.

5. *Eat well.* At this time of emotional and physical depletion, your body needs good nourishment more than ever. If you can only pick at your food, a vitamin supplement might be helpful, but it will not fully make up for a poor diet. Be good to yourself.

6. *Exercise regularly.* Return to your old program or start one as soon as possible. Depression can be lightened a little by the biochemical changes brought by exercise. And you will sleep better. An hour-long walk every day is ideal for many people.

7. *Get rid of imagined guilt.* You did the best you could at the time, all things considered. If you made mistakes, learn to accept that we are all imperfect. Only hindsight is 20-20. If you are convinced that you have *real guilt,* consider professional or spiritual counseling. If you believe in God, a pastor can help you believe also in God's forgiveness.

8. *Accept your understanding of the death,* for the time being. You have probably asked "why?" over and over and have finally realized that you will get no acceptable answer. But you probably have some small degree of understanding. Use that as your viewpoint until you are able to work up to another level of understanding.

9. *Join a group of others who are sorrowing.* Your old circle of friends may change. Even if it does not, you will need new friends who have been through your experience. Bereaved people sometimes form groups for friendship and sharing.

10. *Associate with old friends also.* This may be difficult. Some will be embarrassed by your presence, but they will get over it. If and when you can, talk and act naturally, without avoiding the subject of your loss.

11. *Postpone major decisions.* For example, wait before deciding to sell your house or change jobs.

12. *Record your thoughts in a journal,* if you are inclined at all toward writing. It helps get your feelings out and records your progress.

13. *Turn grief into creative energy.* Find a way to help others. Helping to carry someone else's load is guaranteed to lighten your own. If you have writing ability, use it. Great literature has been written as a tribute to someone loved and lost.

14. *Take advantage of your religious affiliation,* if you have one. If you have been inactive in matters of faith, this might be the time to become involved again. The Bible has much to say about sorrow. Old hymns are relevant. As time passes, you may find you are not so mad at God after all!

15. *Get professional help if needed.* Do not allow crippling grief to continue. There comes a time to stop crying and to live again. Sometimes just a few sessions with a trained counselor will help you to resolve the anger, guilt, and despair that keep you from functioning.

Remember: No matter how deep your sorrow, *you are not alone.* Others have been there and will help share your load if you will let them. Do not deny them the opportunity.

SUGGESTED READING

Kubler-Ross, Elisabeth: *On Death and Dying, Questions on Death and Dying,* and *Death: The Final Stage of Growth,* the first two published by MacMillan, 1969 and 1974, the last by Prentice Hall, 1975. *To Live Until We Say Goodbye,* co-authored with Mel Warshaw, Prentice Hall, 1978, is about the death of the terminally ill. Dr. Kubler-Ross is widely appreciated for her pioneering work in the field.

Marshall, Catherine: *To Live Again,* McGraw-Hill, 1957 (Crest reprint). The author of *A Man Called Peter* writes after the death of her husband.

Lewis, C.S.: *A Grief Observed,* Seabury Press, 1963. Also a Bantam paperback. A famous author writes after the death of his wife.

Schiff, Harriet Sarnoff: *The Bereaved Parent,* Crown Publishers, 1977. Also a Penquin Books paperback. A thorough manual for the grieving parent.

Caine, Lynn: *Widow,* William Morrow & Co., 1974. A frank account of the trauma of widowhood, with realistic suggestions for coping.

Kohn, William K. and Kohn, Jane Burgess: *Widower,* Bacon Press, 1978. A widower relates his personal experiences. Includes comment based on interviews with many other widowers.

If you are a grieving *parent,* I suggest you contact *The Compassionate Friends, Inc.,* P.O. Box 1347, Oak Brook, IL 60521, telephone: (312) 323-5010. There may be a chapter in your area.